JESUS is Alive!

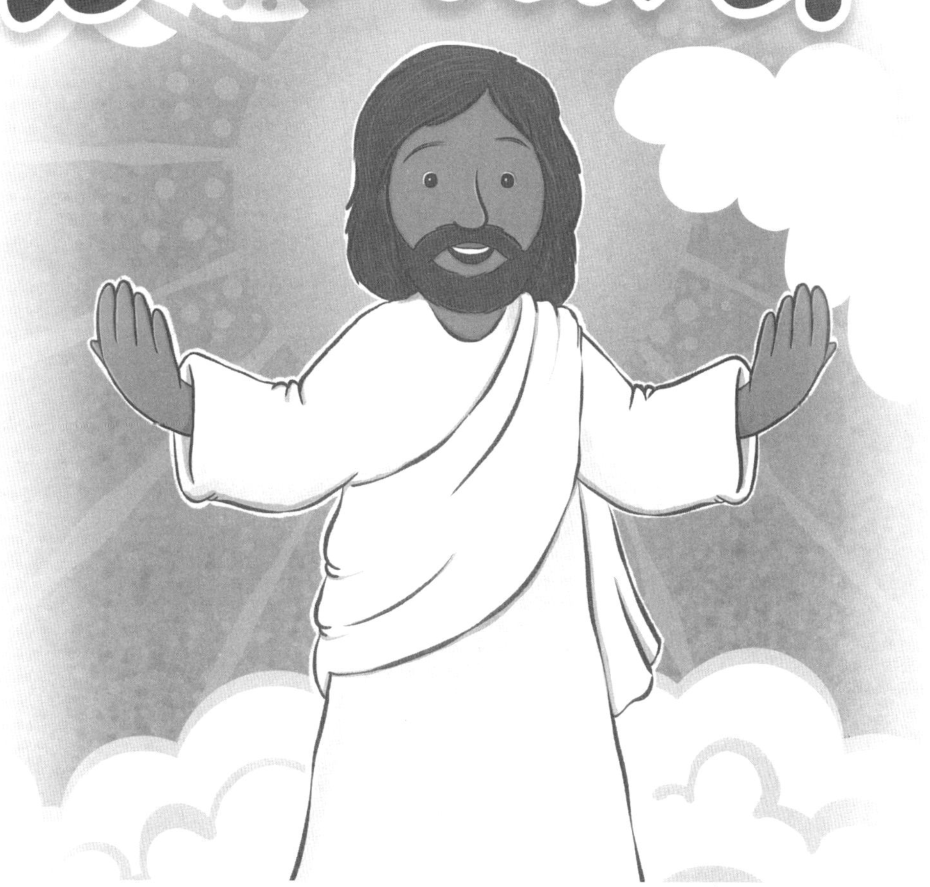

Illustrated by Deb Johnson

305800232025

A long time ago, God made the first people.
He loved them very much.

At first, the people were happy.
They listened to God and did what He said.

Little by little, people forgot about God.
They did mean things. God was sad.

God decided to send His only Son, Jesus, to the world.
Jesus would show people how much God loves them.

Jesus grew up to be a man.

When the time was right, Jesus began teaching the people about God.

Jesus chose 12 men to help Him with His work.
The men were called disciples.

Jesus healed many people who were hurt or sick.

Many people loved Jesus.
They believed what He said about God.

Some men hated Jesus.
They did not believe Jesus when He told them the truth.

The bad men told lies about Jesus.
They took Jesus away and hurt Him.

They nailed Jesus to a cross, and Jesus died.
This was God's plan to save people. Because of Jesus,
God forgives people who are sorry for the bad things they do.

Jesus was buried in a tomb.
The people who loved Jesus were sad.

Three days later, Jesus' friends went to the tomb.
The stone was rolled away. An angel said, "Jesus has risen!"
They were so happy!

Jesus is living with God in heaven now.
If we love Jesus, someday we'll live there too!

God so loved the world that he gave his one and only Son.
John 3:16 (NIV)